MEMORIAL DAY

HOLIDAYS

Lynda Sorensen

The Rourke Press, Inc.
Vero Beach, Florida 32964

Edited by Sandra A. Robinson

PHOTO CREDITS
© James P. Rowan: pages 4, 7, 12, 15; © Frank Balthis: cover;
© Lynn M. Stone: title page, pages 13, 18; © Emil Punter/Photo Vision:
page 8; © Gene Ahrens: page 17; courtesy U.S. Army Military History
Institute: pages 10, 21

Library of Congress Cataloging-in-Publication Data

Sorensen, Lynda, 1953-
   Memorial day / Lynda Sorensen.
      p. cm. — (Holidays)
   Includes index.
   ISBN 1-57103-071-9
   1. Memorial Day—Juvenile literature. I. Title.
II. Series: Sorensen, Lynda, 1953-   Holidays.
E642.S68   1994
394.2'684—dc20   94-17722
                                                      CIP
                                                      AC
Printed in the USA

TABLE OF CONTENTS

MEMORIAL DAY

Memorial Day honors the men and women of the American Army, Navy, Coast Guard, Air Force and Marines who died while serving their country.

Memorial Day is a **national** holiday in the United States. It is celebrated on either May 30 or 31.

Memorial Day began as a holiday to remember the American soldiers who died in the Civil War (1861-1865). As more wars were fought, it became a day for Americans to honor and remember their dead from all wars.

Thousands of Americans who served in the U.S. Armed Services are buried in Arlington National Cemetery, Virginia

THE FIRST MEMORIAL DAY

Hundreds of thousands of Americans lost family members and friends in the Civil War — the war fought between the Northern and Southern states. After the war ended, people wanted a special way to remember the brave soldiers who died. On May 5, 1866, the village of Waterloo, New York, held a ceremony to honor their Civil War dead.

One hundred years later, the U.S. **Congress** officially named Waterloo as the birthplace of the Memorial Day holiday.

Memorial Day began as a way to honor soldiers who died in the Civil War, shown here in a battle re-enactment

DECORATION DAY

After the Civil War, former Northern soldiers founded a **veterans'** organization called the Grand Army of the Republic (GAR). Members of the GAR held a special ceremony on May 30, 1868, to decorate the graves of Northern soldiers.

The ceremonies were repeated each year. The day became known as Decoration Day. The official name was changed to Memorial Day in 1882.

Memorial Day ceremonies began with the holiday known as Decoration Day

CELEBRATIONS IN THE SOUTH

Because Memorial Day began as a holiday to remember Northern soldiers, several Southern states still celebrate their own memorial days. They honor the soldiers who died fighting for the South, which had formed the Confederate States of America during the Civil War. In Virginia, for example, the last Monday in May is Confederate Memorial Day. Texas celebrates Confederate Heroes Day on January 19.

Dead Confederate soldiers lie at the edge of Rose's Woods after the Battle of Gettysburg in 1863

The Vietnam Veterans Memorial in Washington, D.C., honors the American soldiers who died in Vietnam

The bronze statue "Spirit of American Youth Rising from the Waves" by Donald DeLue honors the nearly 10,000 U.S. soldiers who died in the attack on German positions in France in June, 1944

GETTYSBURG NATIONAL MILITARY PARK

One of the worst battles of the Civil War was fought at Gettysburg, Pennsylvania, in 1863. Thousands of brave men from the North and the South died during the terrible fighting. President Abraham Lincoln made part of the battlefield a cemetery.

Today the **site** is Gettysburg National Military Park. Each Memorial Day, ceremonies at Gettysburg honor those brave soldiers of long ago.

Gettysburg National Military Park in Gettysburg, Pennsylvania, is the site of a major Civil War battle

ARLINGTON NATIONAL CEMETERY

Arlington National Cemetery in Arlington, Virginia, is the final resting place for thousands of American soldiers. An American soldier from each of four wars — World War I, World War II, the Korean War and the Vietnam War — is buried in Arlington's Tomb of the Unknowns. They are soldiers who were never identified and remain "known but to God."

Each Memorial Day, a ceremony is held at the Tomb of the Unknowns. An honor guard of American soldiers places a wreath on the tomb, and a bugle sounds the clear, sad notes of taps.

American soldiers from four wars are buried in the Tomb of the Unknowns at Arlington National Cemetery, Virginia

VETERANS' GROUPS

The American Legion and Veterans of Foreign Wars (VFW) are large organizations of U.S. veterans. Veterans are former soldiers — the men and women of America's Air Force, Army, Navy, Coast Guard and Marines. Some veterans who fought as long ago as World War I (1914-1918) are still living today.

Members of veterans' groups help organize Memorial Day ceremonies and take part in those events. Veterans' groups also help care for **disabled** veterans and the families of veterans who have died.

The American Legion plays a big part
in organizing Memorial Day ceremonies

REMEMBERING

America takes time out on Memorial Day to honor the memory and sacrifice of its dead heroes. Do you know how many Americans have died in battle since the Civil War?

Over 115,000 American soldiers died in Europe during World War I. More than 400,000 Americans died in World War II, which was fought in many parts of the world, including the Aleutian Islands of Alaska.

Together the Korean War (1950-1953) and the Vietnam War (1965-1973) took the lives of more than 100,000 American soldiers.

American soldiers look for enemy soldiers while on patrol in Vietnam in 1967

CELEBRATING MEMORIAL DAY

Many special Memorial Day programs help living Americans remember those who died in war.

Towns and cities throughout the United States hold parades with marching bands, veterans and soldiers. Americans decorate veterans' graves with wreaths, flowers and flags.

On Memorial Day, with ceremony and prayerful silence, America honors the brave veterans it lost in battle.

Glossary

Congress (KAHN gress) — in the United States, a group of lawmakers representing the states

disabled (dis A buld) — unable to perform certain tasks because of permanent injury or illness; handicapped

national (NAH shun ul) — of or relating to a nation

site (SITE) — a piece of land used for a specific purpose, such as a battle; a place where something happened

veteran (VEH ter in) — a former soldier; a man or a woman who served in the armed forces, for example, America's Air Force, Army, Navy, Coast Guard or Marines

INDEX